The Magic of Standards

EIGHT PIANO SOLOS ARRANGED BY JEREMY SISKIND

CONTENTS

ISBN 978-1-4768-7434-0

HAL•LEONARD®
CORPORATION
7777 W. BLUEMOUND RD. P.O. BOX 13819 MILWAUKEE, WI 53213

Visit Hal Leonard Online at
www.halleonard.com

Bewitched
from PAL JOEY

Words by Lorenz Hart
Music by Richard Rodgers
Arranged by Jeremy Siskind

Ballad, freely (♩ = 61)

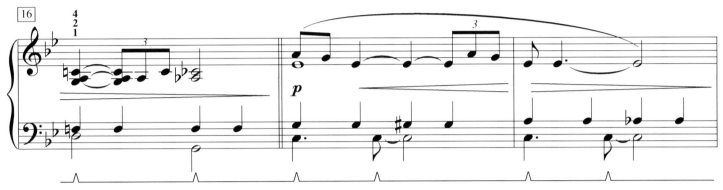

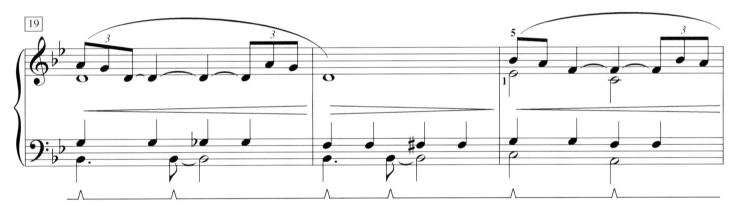

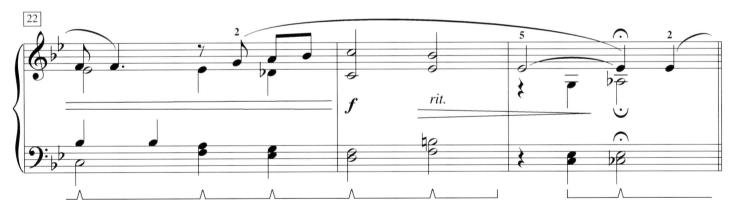

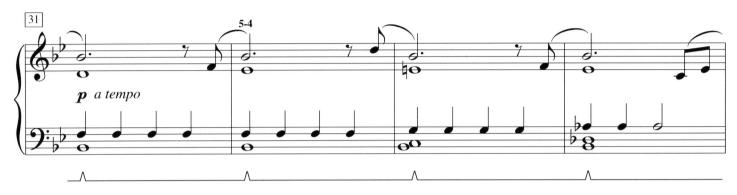

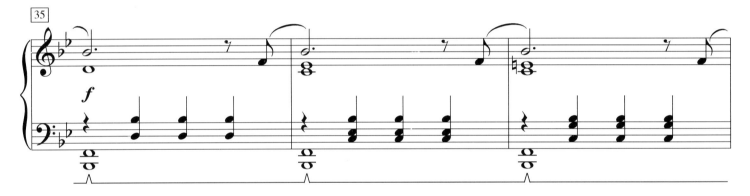

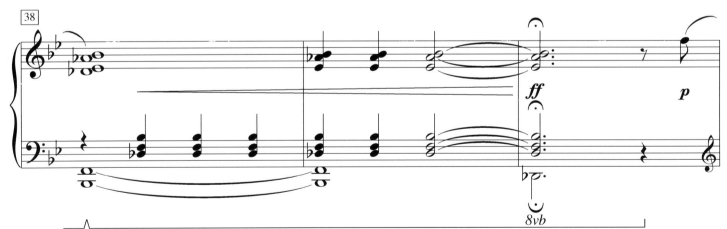

Chelsea Bridge

By Billy Strayhorn
Arranged by Jeremy Siskind

Slowly, with mystery (♩ = 60)

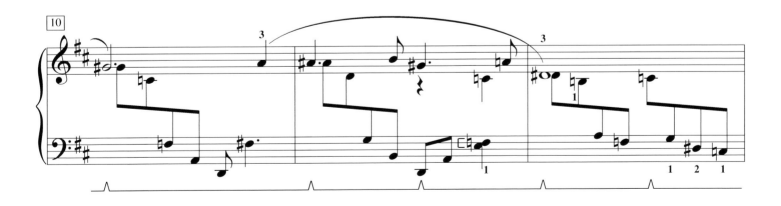

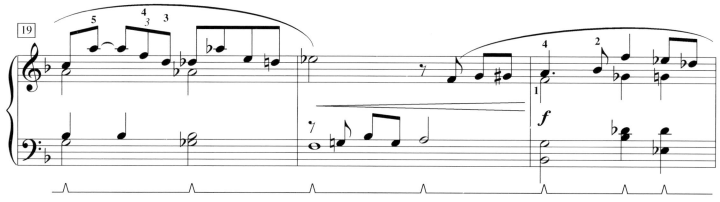

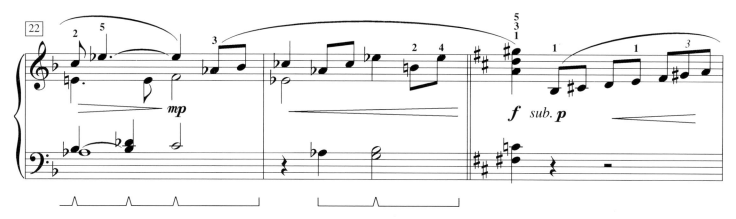

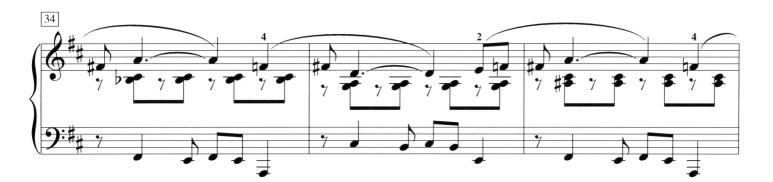

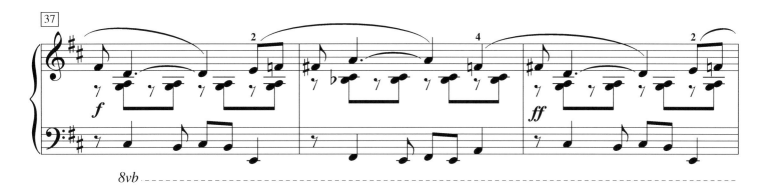

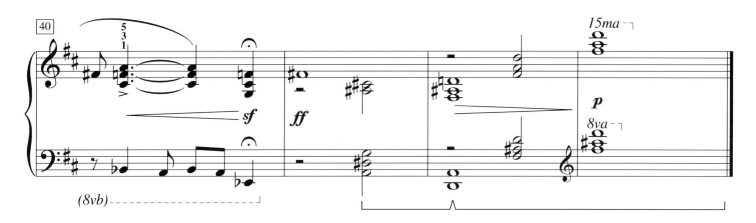

7

The Girl from Ipanema
(Garôta De Ipanema)

Music by Antonio Carlos Jobim
English Words by Norman Gimbel
Original Words by Vinicius de Moraes
Arranged by Jeremy Siskind

Loosely and Fluidly (♩ = 117)

una corda throughout

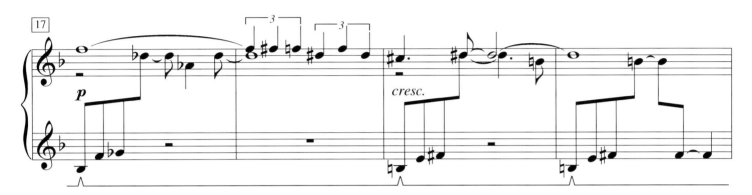

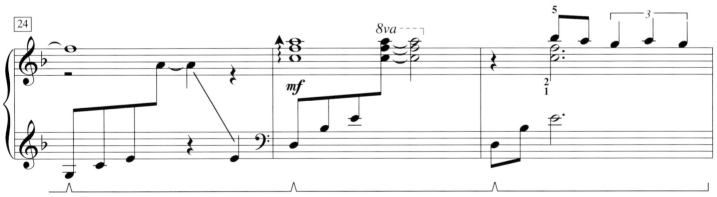

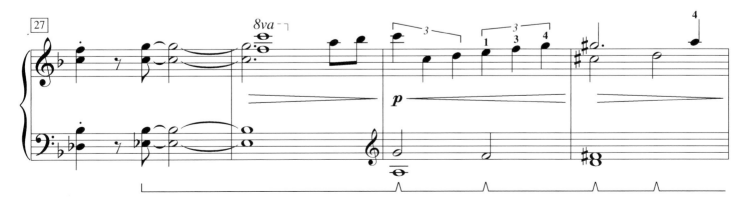

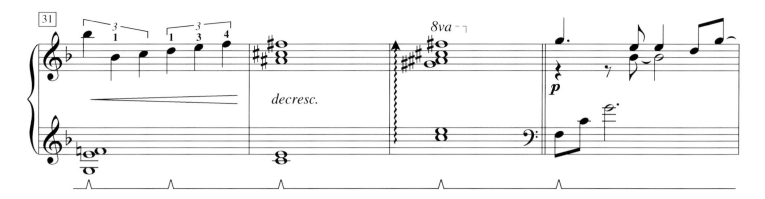

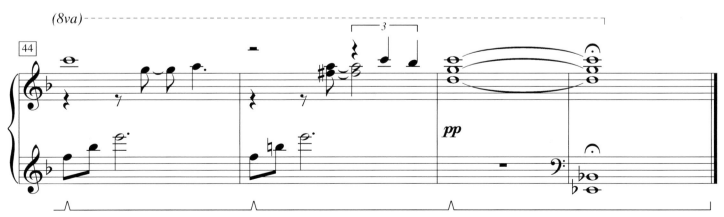

I'm Beginning to See the Light

Words and Music by Don George,
Johnny Hodges, Duke Ellington
and Harry James
Arranged by Jeremy Siskind

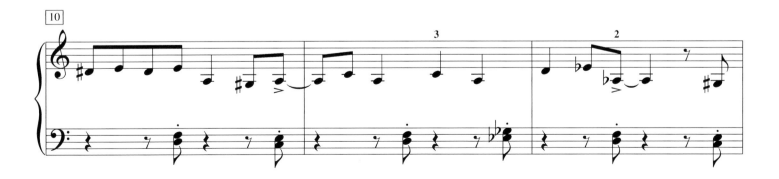

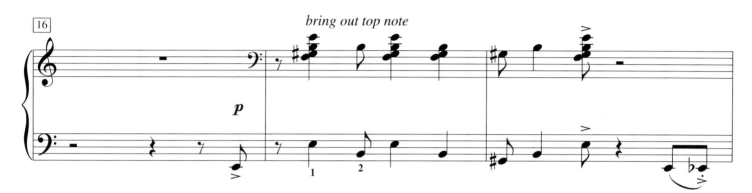

bring out top note

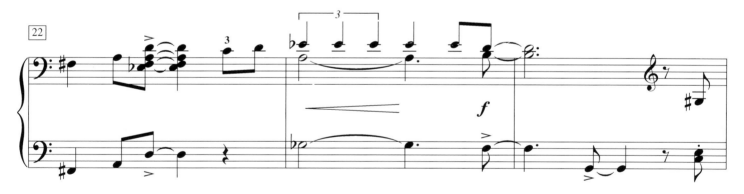

slinky, with a groove; bring out the top note

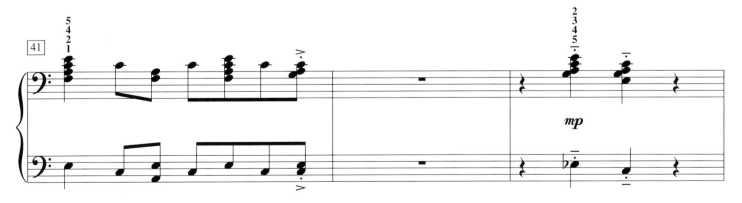

13

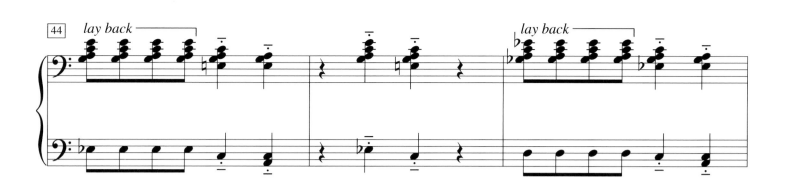

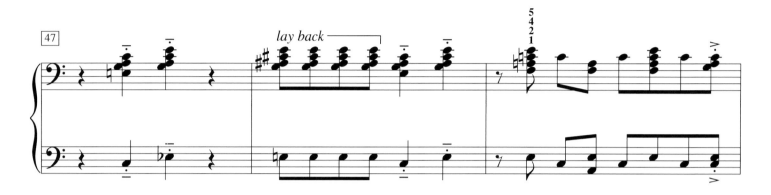

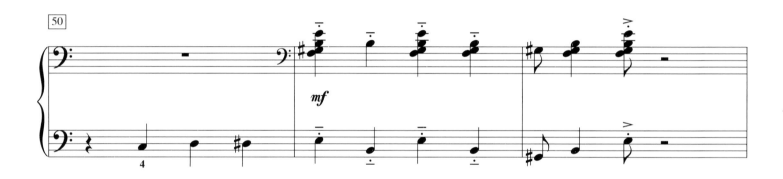

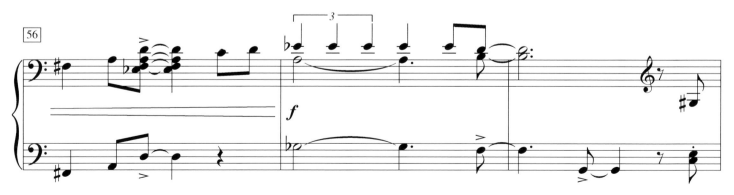

Laura

Lyrics by Johnny Mercer
Music by David Raksin
Arranged by Jeremy Siskind

Ballad, rubato (♩ = 72)

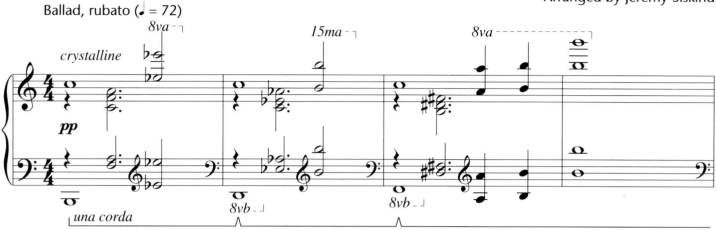

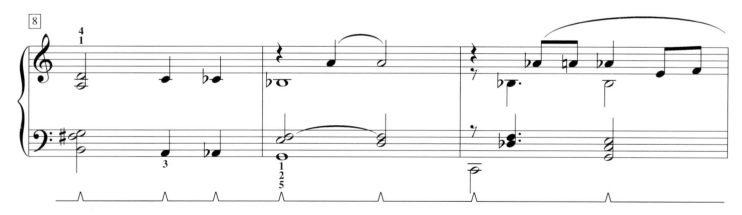

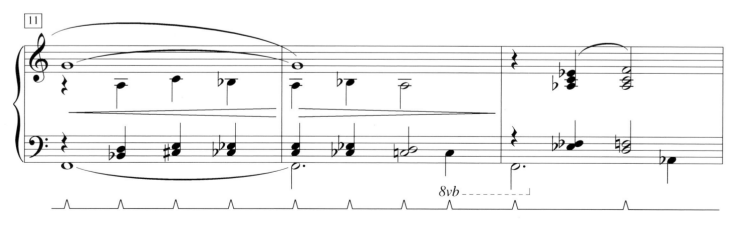

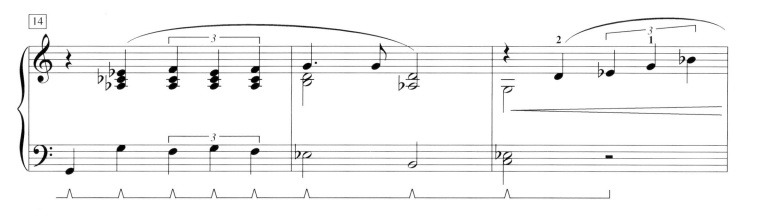

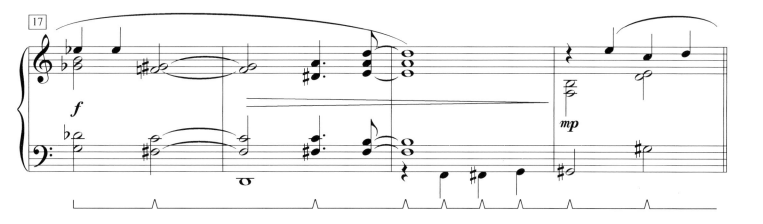

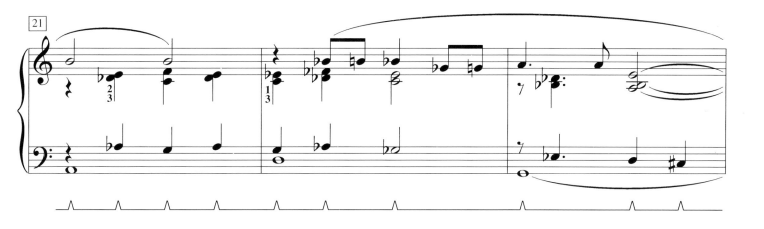

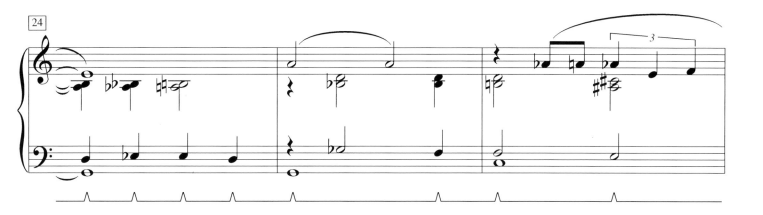

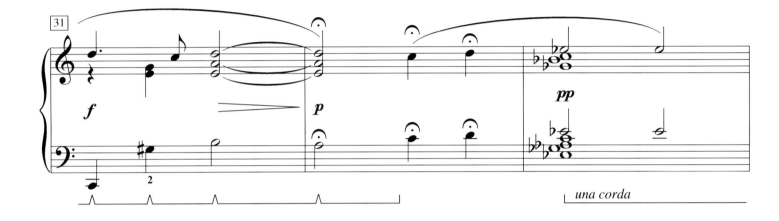

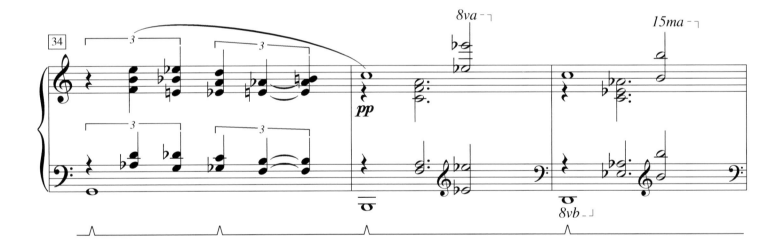

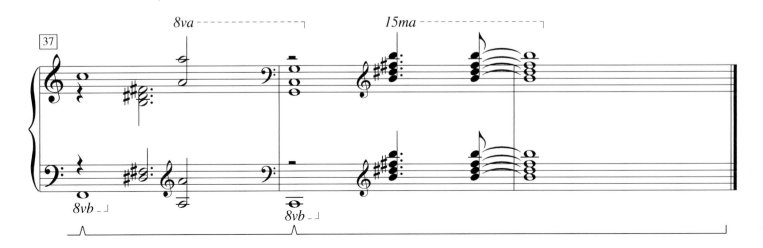

Lulu's Back in Town

Words by Al Dubin
Music by Harry Warren
Arranged by Jeremy Siskind

Fast Swing! (♩ = 190)

Solo

mf

Play L.H. bass with sharp accents
8vb

(8vb)

(8vb)

(8vb)

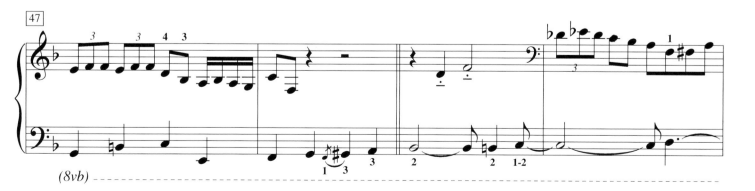

(8vb)

(8vb)

(8vb)

(8vb)

ff

(8vb)

straight eighths

Puttin' on the Ritz

from the Motion Picture PUTTIN' ON THE RITZ

Words and Music by
Irving Berlin
Arranged by Jeremy Siskind

Fast Swing (♩ = 184)

mf

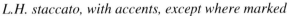

L.H. staccato, with accents, except where marked

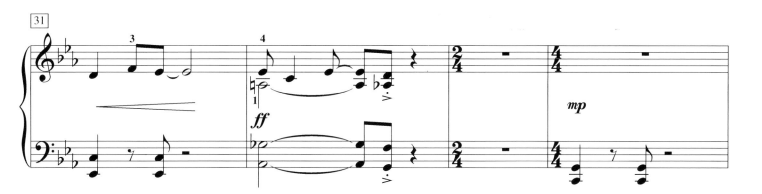

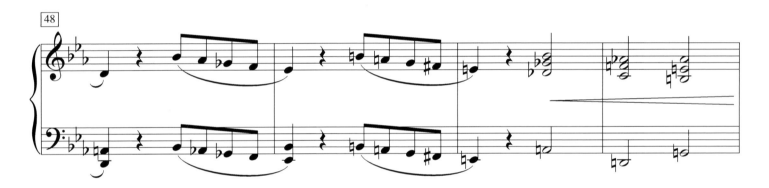

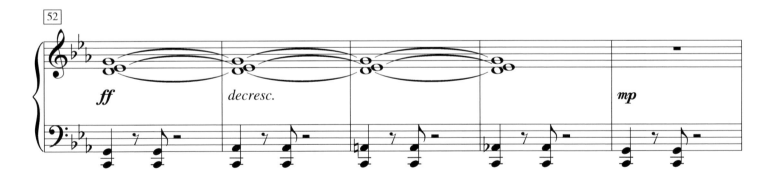

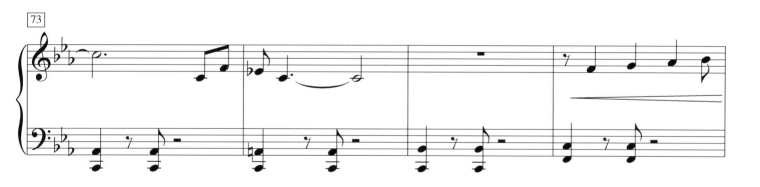

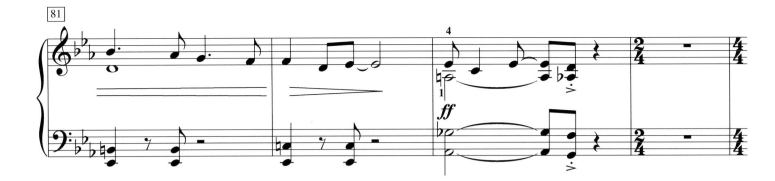

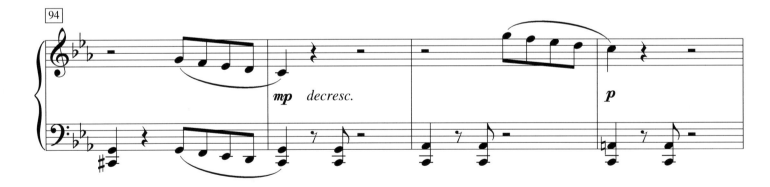

Wouldn't It Be Loverly

from MY FAIR LADY

Lyrics by Alan Jay Lerner
Music by Frederick Loewe
Arranged by Jeremy Siskind

Wistfully (♩ = 68)

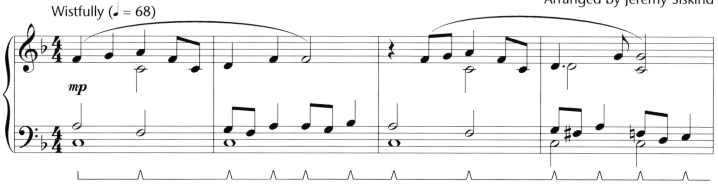

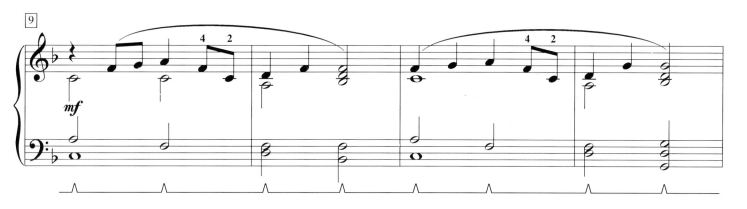

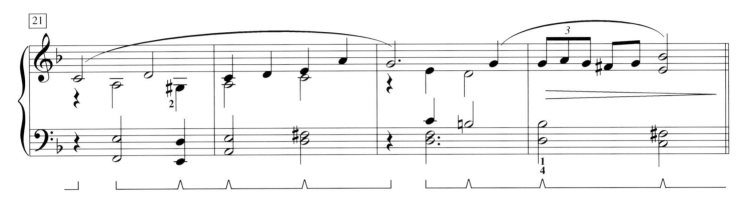

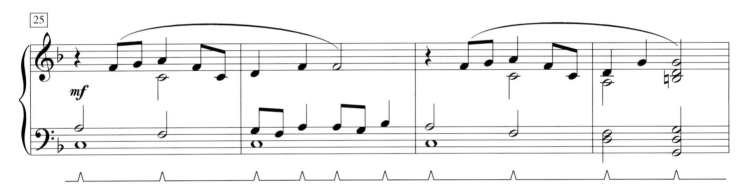

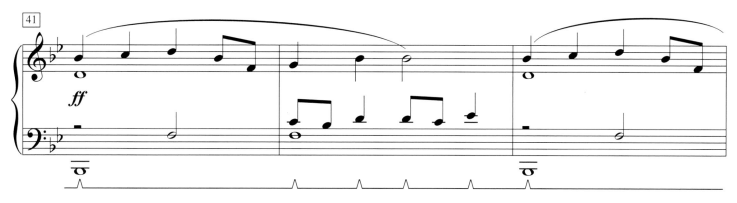

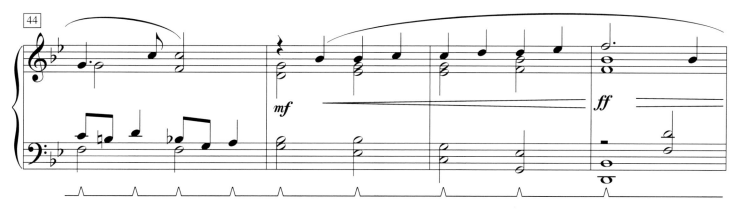

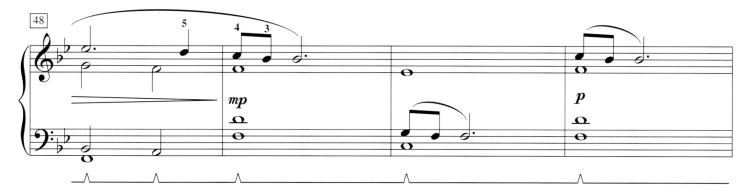

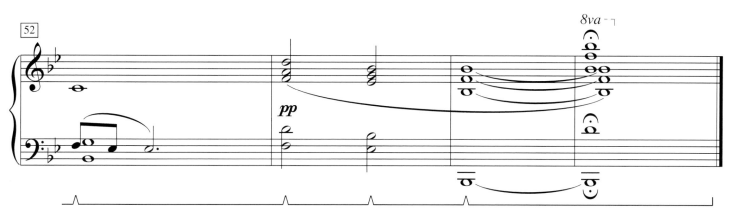

Expand Your Jazz Piano Technique

BLUES, JAZZ & ROCK RIFFS FOR KEYBOARDS
by William T. Eveleth
Because so much of today's popular music has its roots in blues, the material included here is a vital component of jazz, rock, R&B, gospel, soul, and even pop. The author has compiled actual licks, riffs, turnaround phrases, embellishments, and basic patterns that define good piano blues and can be used as a basis for players to explore and create their own style.
00221028 Book...$11.95

BOOGIE WOOGIE FOR BEGINNERS
by Frank Paparelli
This bestseller is now available with a CD of demonstration tracks! A short easy method for learning to play boogie woogie, designed for the beginner and average pianist. Includes: exercises for developing left-hand bass; 25 popular boogie woogie bass patterns; arrangements of "Down the Road a Piece" and "Answer to the Prayer" by well-known pianists; a glossary of musical terms for dynamics, tempo and style; and more.
00312559 Book/CD Pack................................$14.99

A CLASSICAL APPROACH TO JAZZ PIANO IMPROVISATION
by Dominic Alldis
This keyboard instruction book is designed for the person who was trained classically but wants to expand into the very exciting — yet very different — world of jazz improvisation. Author Dominic Alldis provides clear explanations and musical examples of: pentatonic improvisation; the blues; rock piano; rhythmic placement; scale theory; major, minor and pentatonic scale theory applications; and more.
00310979 Book..$16.95

THE HARMONY OF BILL EVANS
by Jack Reilly
A compilation of articles — now revised and expanded — that originally appeared in the quarterly newsletter *Letter from Evans*, this unique folio features extensive analysis of Evans' work. Pieces examined include: B Minor Waltz • Funny Man • How Deep Is the Ocean • I Fall in Love Too Easily • I Should Care • Peri's Scope • Time Remembered • and Twelve Tone Tune.
00699405 Book..$19.99

THE HARMONY OF BILL EVANS - VOLUME 2
by Jack Reilly
Reilly's second volume includes two important theory chapters, plus ten of Bill's most passionate and melodically gorgeous works. The accompanying audio CD will add to the enjoyment, understanding, and appreciation of the written examples. Songs include: For Nenette • January • Laurie • Maxine • Song for Helen • Turn Out the Stars • Very Early • Waltz for Debby • and more.
00311828 Book/CD Pack................................$29.99

AN INTRODUCTION TO JAZZ CHORD VOICING FOR KEYBOARD - 2ND EDITION
by Bill Boyd
This book is designed for the pianist/keyboardist with moderate technical skills and reading ability who desires to play jazz styles and learn to improvise from reading chord symbols. It is an ideal self-teaching book for keyboardists in high school and junior high jazz ensembles. Unique features of this book include chords and progressions written out in all keys, a simple fingering system which applies to all keys, and coverage of improvising and solo playing.
00854100 Book/CD Pack................................$19.95

INTROS, ENDINGS & TURNAROUNDS FOR KEYBOARD
ESSENTIAL PHRASES FOR SWING, LATIN, JAZZ WALTZ, AND BLUES STYLES
by John Valerio
Learn the intros, endings and turnarounds that all of the pros know and use! This new keyboard instruction book by John Valerio covers swing styles, ballads, Latin tunes, jazz waltzes, blues, major and minor keys, vamps and pedal tones, and more.
00290525 Book..$12.95

JAZZ ETUDE INSPIRATIONS
EIGHT PIANO ETUDES INSPIRED BY THE MASTERS
by Jeremy Siskind
Etudes in the style of legendary greats Oscar Peterson, Duke Ellington, McCoy Tyner, Jelly Roll Morton, Chick Corea, Brad Mehldau, Count Basie and Herbie Hancock will help students master some technical challenges posed by each artist's individual style. The performance notes include a biography, practice tips and a list of significant recordings. Tunes include: Count on Me • Hand Battle • Jelly Roll Me Home • Minor Tyner • Oscar's Bounce • Pineapple Woman • Repeat After Me • Tears Falling on Still Water.
00296860 Book...$8.99

JAZZ PIANO
by Liam Noble
Featuring lessons, music, historical analysis and rare photos, this book/CD pack provides a complete overview of the techniques and styles popularized by 15 of the greatest jazz pianists of all time. All the best are here: from the early ragtime stylings of Ferdinand "Jelly Roll" Morton, to the modal escapades of Bill Evans, through the '70s jazz funk of Herbie Hancock. CD contains 15 full-band tracks.
00311050 Book/CD Pack................................$19.99

JAZZ PIANO CONCEPTS & TECHNIQUES
by John Valerio
This book provides a step-by-step approach to learning basic piano realizations of jazz and pop tunes from lead sheets. Systems for voicing chords are presented from the most elementary to the advanced along with methods for practicing each system. Both the non-jazz and the advanced jazz player will benefit from the focus on: chords, chord voicings, harmony, melody and accompaniment, and styles.
00290490 Book..$18.99

JAZZ PIANO TECHNIQUE
by John Valerio
This one-of-a-kind book applies traditional technique exercises to specific jazz piano needs. Topics include: scales (major, minor, chromatic, pentatonic, etc.), arpeggios (triads, seventh chords, upper structures), finger independence exercises (static position, held notes, Hanon exercises), and more! The audio includes 45 recorded examples.
00312059 Book/Online Audio.....................$19.99

JAZZ PIANO VOICINGS
by Rob Mullins
Long-time performer and educator Rob Mullins helps players enter the jazz world by providing voicings that will help the player develop skills in the jazz genre and start sounding professional right away — without years of study! Includes a "Numeric Voicing Chart," chord indexes in all 12 keys, info about what range of the instrument you can play chords in, and a beginning approach to bass lines.
00310914 Book..$19.95

HAL•LEONARD® CORPORATION
7777 W. BLUEMOUND RD. P.O. BOX 13819 MILWAUKEE, WI 53213
www.halleonard.com

1015